WRITTEN BY JOHN EATON ILLUSTRATED BY JULIA VASINA

Spid the Spider Helps Save the Planet

First published as a paperback in 2023

ISBN 978-1-915376-06-0

Audiobook 978-1-915376-08-4

eBook 978-1-915376-07-7

Published by Spidling Productions Ltd
Meadow Court, Minehead Road, Taunton, Somerset, TA2 6NS, England

British Library Cataloguing in Publication Data

Eaton, John, Spid the Spider Helps Save the Planet

Printed and bound in Great Britain by Biddles Ltd, King's Lynn, Norfolk

This book is printed on acid-free paper responsibly manufactured from sustainable forestry in which at least two trees are planted for each one used in paper production.

Website: www.spidthespider.com
Email: spid@spidthespider.com
Facebook: www.facebook.com/ spidthespider
Instagram: www.instagram.com/ spidthespider
Twitter: www.twitter.com/ spidthespider
YouTube: www.youtube.com/ spidthespider
TikTok: tiktok.com/ Its_Spid_The_Spider

With grateful thanks to my wife Sue, Peter Dymond, Angus Scott, Melissa Shephard (for her original illustrations), Michael Smetham, Alexa Tewkesbury, Guy Tomlinson, Julia Vasina, Chrissie Venn, Alistair Whiteley and Alexa Whitten.

And especially to my granddaughter Evaleigh, without whom, Spid would not exist.

THIS BOOK FEATURES:

HELLO SPIDLINGS!

Spid the spider here. I live in a village called Spider Webdon, which has its own steam train station. I can go almost anywhere when it's open. It's spidtastic.

The bus service is rubbish though and there are no buses at all on Spundays.

My house is at the top of a hill. I live there on my own and I work *very* hard for *very* little pay. Which isn't helpful when you're trying to improve your prospects.

I like listening to music called SpidRap and I've got a girlfriend called Bid. One day, I'd like to marry Bid – *if* I ever earn enough money to get married.

I do try hard to be good. I want to be a better spidling. But sometimes ... well ... let's just say I get a bit carried away. That's when Bid has to put me straight. She's clever at that.

And did I mention I write songs? I've written some about the adventures I have in my books. I sing them too. If you have a listen, you can join in and sing along ...

It was a quiet Splatterday in Spider Webdon.

Spid came down from his morning shower to find that the roads were quiet; the weather was quiet; even the birds were quiet.

In fact, the only sound Spid could hear was the music playing quietly on his radio.

"This, Spid," Spid said to himself, "is the perfect sort of Splatterday morning to go for a walk. A quiet walk is exactly what you need. It'll help you unwind after another busy week at work. Emm, emm." So, he switched off his radio, stepped outside, and whistled a tune as he set off down his garden path.

But before Spid had even reached his gate, disaster struck.

SQUELCH …

Spid's foot landed on something squidgy and shot out from under him. As he crashed to the ground with … well … a ***CRASH,*** his hand landed hard on an empty Arachno-Cola can. The metal cut into him.

"Ow!" Spid wailed, nursing a sore finger. He glared at the now flat can. Then he twisted round to glare at whatever it was that had **SQUELCHED** and caused him to slip over.

"What??" he snarled, leaning towards the "thing" to get a better look. "If that isn't a half-eaten Waspburger, then I'm a stag beetle. And I'm not a stag beetle so that's definitely a half-eaten Waspburger – which someone has thrown into my garden!"

With a grumpy grunt, Spid scrambled to his feet. "Waspburgers and Arachno-Cola cans," he muttered. "Spidlings throwing *their* litter in *my* garden. Disgusting!" He snatched up the can and stomped back up the garden path to put it in his recycling bin.

However, as Spid stomped, something behind him didn't feel quite right. He reached round, and found a greasy McSpid's Waspburger box stuck to his bottom.

"Well, Spid," he grumbled, "if that isn't the absolute spidding limit. What do other spidlings think your garden is? A rubbish tip?"

With that, he threw the cardboard Waspburger box into the recycling bin, along with the Arachno-Cola can. Then he marched back into his house and slammed the door.

And that's my Splatterday ruined, he thought. *All I wanted was to enjoy a quiet walk on a quiet morning. Now, thanks to those litter-spids, I'm too cross to enjoy anything.*

His nose suddenly wrinkled. *Not only that,* his thoughts went on, *I now stink of old burgers. I shall have to go and have a shower and I've only just had one!*

After his shower, Spid's cut finger felt better. Spid himself, however, didn't feel any better at all.

"You know what you need, Spid," he said to himself. "You need to put your feet up with a soothing cup of Earl Moth tea and read the newspaper. The *Spider Times* is bound to have some interesting news. That'll take your mind off the litter-spids who've ruined your Splatterday morning."

SPIDER TIMES
Own Goal
SPIDER TIMES
Planet Problems

But when Spid sat down in his armchair, took a comforting sip of hot Earl Moth tea and picked up his copy of the *Spider Times*, he was horrified. The front-page story was all about the damage being caused to the world and everything in it.

First, Spid read how air pollution was making the planet heat up. This was having a bad effect on the weather and the way things worked in nature.

Next, he read how it wasn't just air pollution that was causing a problem. The land and the water were being polluted too – with rubbish! He read about all the plastic that ended up in the sea and how dangerous it was for the fish and the seabirds. There was so much plastic in one particular ocean called the Pacific, that it had joined together to become two huge islands of plastic known as the Great Pacific Garbage Patch.

6
Countryside in chaos
Litter adversely affects the environment. Littering along the road,
billion tons of debris enter the world's oceans annually and most of it is long-lasting plastic.[2] Litter also reduces air quality due to the smell and toxic/chemical vapor emanating from the trash. A polluted environment can encourage the spread of diseases. Toxic chemicals and disease-causing microorganisms in the trash may also contaminate water systems and spread water-borne diseases which can negatively affect the health of both animals and humans if unclean or untreated water is
Plastic litter is another threat to the environment and its inhabitants. It has often been mistaken for food by both land and marine wildlife. When consumed by animals, they reduce the stomach capacity since they cannot be digested. In the long-term it affects the animals' eating habits, eventually killing the animals. Much of marine wildlife including birds,
whales, dolphins and turtles have been found dead with plastic and cigarettes found in their stomachs.[4] An estimated 100,000 sea mammals are killed by plastic litter every year.[5] Some of the materials may also be poisonous or contain sharp objects therefore damaging the animal's vital organs or severely injuring them. Another negative aspect of
littering is that it is too expensive for a country, society and individuals. Cleaning up litter requires a huge amount of money that is financed by taxpayers that could be used in more productive ways. Littered places are visually displeasing and they depreciate the aesthetic and real value of the surrounding environments. Places with large amounts of litter are often
7

The news was no better when Spid turned the page. There were pictures of litter everywhere. Cans, bottles and food packaging had just been thrown away in the streets. Old armchairs and televisions had been dumped in hedgerows, spoiling the countryside. It was causing dreadful problems for wildlife and doing terrible things to Spiddle Earth.

Far from enjoying his cup of tea, Spid didn't even want it anymore. He let it go cold.

As he carried on reading, he came to an article about recycling. It said that if every spidling in Spidland recycled all their copies of the *Spider Times*, that paper could be used again. This would save thousands and thousands of trees.

That's a spidtastic number, Spid thought to himself. *Because obviously trees are where paper comes from.*

When Spid had read the newspaper from cover to cover, he made sure to put it in his paper-recycling bin. But it didn't make him feel good.

This morning, I was upset about the litter in my garden, he couldn't help thinking. *But that tiny bit of litter isn't even a millionth ... a trillionth ... a gazillionth of the problem. And I can't just sit here and not try to do something about it.*

So Spid stopped sitting and jumped up out of his armchair. He paced this way and that. That way and this.

"Come on, Spid, think, think!" he said to himself.

And Spid thought, thought. But no matter how much he tried to come up with a plan to help the environment, he just didn't have any ideas.
The problem seemed ***too big.***

All of a sudden, his eyes lit up. "Of course! You know who'll help, don't you, Spid? Your best friend, Herman the Harvestman. He spends his days helping Farmer Spidcrop in the fields. He knows lots about the environment and how to take care of it. He'll tell you what to do. I don't know why you didn't think of him before."

Straightaway, Spid picked up his phone and dialled Herman's number.

"Hello?" said Herman's voice when he answered.

"It's Spid," said Spid.

"Are you having a good Splatterday, Spid?" Herman asked.

"No, I am not!" huffed Spid. "I slipped on a Waspburger, cut my finger on an Arachno-Cola can and got a McSpid's burger box stuck to my bottom. And that was only in my garden. Then I read about climate change in the *Spider Times* and how all our rubbish is having a terrible effect on the planet. *Then* I tried to come up with a plan to do something about it – a *plan* for the *planet*, you might say – but I couldn't think of anything. So now I'm ringing you."

"Oh dear," Herman replied. "I've never had a burger box stuck to my bottom but I can imagine it's not very nice. I did once sit on an ant, I seem to remember. It was very tickly. I'm not sure who was more put out – the ant or me."

But Spid hadn't rung Herman to talk about tickly ants, whether they were put out or not. "The thing is, Herman, we've got to do something. And *you* know how to look after the environment. It's what you do and it's what you care about. I need your help to come up with a *plan* for the *planet*."

"Hmm ..." Herman thought for a moment. "Just us on our own coming up with a plan for the entire planet could be tricky. The planet is huge and we're very small. But, if everyone everywhere looked after their tiny little bit of it, that would make all the difference."

"So what you're saying is, if we look after Spider Webdon and get rid of all our rubbish properly, that's one little piece of the planet we can help. And the more pieces that get help, the better the planet will become."

"That's it exactly," said Herman. "I'm quite surprised I managed to explain it so clearly."

"Oh, it's very clear," Spid replied. "Put the kettle on, Herman. Emm, emm. I'll get the gang together and we'll be right over. Today's the day we say, 'No more littering!' to the litter-spids of Spider Webdon. It has to stop before they turn the town into the ***Giant Spider Webdon Rubbish Dump***!"

At Herman's house, Spid, Bid, Cleverley Evaleigh, Rid, Stid, and of course Herman stood round his kitchen table.

Cleverley Evaleigh had planned to spend her Splatterday building herself a new computer. But – "Please, *please* come," Spid had said. "We need ideas and none of us are as cleverley as you are, Cleverley Evaleigh."

Cleverley Evaleigh liked it when Spid told her how cleverley she was. So she'd shoved all the computer bits and pieces back under her bed and hurried round to Herman's house.

"Did you put the kettle on, Herman?" asked Spid.

"I did," said Herman.

"And are we having a cup of Earl Moth tea?" asked Spid.

"No," said Herman. "Because I don't have any Earl Moth teabags. In fact, I don't have any tea at all. I don't really like it, to tell you the truth."

Spid frowned. "Then why did you put the kettle on?"

"Because you told me to," Herman replied.

Bid smiled. "Never mind, Herman. We don't need tea to help us stop litter-spids in Spider Webdon. But we do need ideas. Have you got any?"

"As a matter of fact, I have. And if we all work together, those litter-spids will learn to think twice before dropping their rubbish anywhere they feel like it.

"At the moment," Herman went on, "some spidlings seem to think it's all right to drop litter on the streets instead of using rubbish or recycling bins. Car drivers throw litter out of their car windows. Picnickers and ramblers leave their rubbish in parks and on our beautiful hillsides, instead of taking it home to throw away in their own bins.

“And that’s not all. What about fly-tippers?”

Rid and Stid looked at each other. “Fly-tippers?” said Stid. “Are there spidlings who actually tip flies onto the sides of the road?”

Rid shook his head. "No, I don't believe it. I've never seen piles of flies anywhere. Or heard any. After all, a pile of flies would make a lot of buzzing."

"No, no," said Bid, "fly-tipping has nothing to do with buzzing flies. When anyone dumps large amounts of rubbish anywhere it's not supposed to be – that's called fly-tipping. Things like old chairs and sofas. Instead of taking them to proper rubbish dumps, some spidlings fly-tip and leave them in field gateways or hedges. That creates more work for farmers because they then have to spend time getting rid of it. It's dangerous for wildlife too."

"Exactly," Herman said. "Then there's all the rubbish thrown into our rivers, which ends up in the sea. The plastic harms fish when they eat it. Then it harms other sea creatures and people when *they* eat the fish."

Cleverley Evaleigh looked sad. "How awful," she said. "I never knew all this, Herman. So the problem's much bigger than just Spider Webdon."

"It is," Herman replied. "But Spider Webdon is our local town, so that's where we start to make a difference. And how we're going to make a difference today is by catching litter-spids actually doing some littering."

Spid looked doubtful. "How are we going to do that? Some spidlings are fast. Really fast. I'm *quite* fast but I'm not sure I could catch a litter-spid if they ran off when they saw me chasing them."

"We don't have to chase anybody," Herman explained. "Which is just as well because I've been known to fall over when I try to run fast. No – we're going to hide in the bushes on the little roundabout on the edge of town. From there, we'll be able to take pictures and videos of litter-spids chucking rubbish out of their car windows as they drive by."

"***Spidtastic idea!***" Spid exclaimed. "We'll catch them in the act." He thought the idea was even more spidtastic because it meant he didn't have to run anywhere.

"Then," Herman went on, "we can put all the photos and videos together and make some kind of film with them to send to newspapers. That's how to let people know there's a problem – get the papers to report on it. Then perhaps something can be done about it."

"An even more *spidtastic idea!*" Spid cried. "How do we put everything together to make the film?"

"Don't ask me," said Herman. "I'm just an ideas-spid."

Cleverley Evaleigh bounced up and down with excitement. "I know exactly how to do it."

Spid beamed. "I knew we could rely on you. You're so cleverley, Cleverley Evaleigh."

Not to be outdone, Bid said, "I've got a clever idea too. Would you like to hear it?"

"Of course," Spid replied. "The more clever ideas the better. There's a lot of littering to stop."

"Well, then, you could write a song," Bid said. "It could tell people what a sorry state the planet is in and that they need to start taking action to help it. Then your song could be the music that goes with the film."

Spid's smile stretched even wider. "Bid, you're brilliant! I *will* write a song. Right here and now. Emm, emm. Then it'll be ready for when Cleverley Evaleigh has finished putting the film together."

So Spid wrote the song. Right there and then. And here it is ...

PLAN-IT EARTH

Oh, the water's brown,
And the sky is falling down.
The gypsy king has lost his crown,
Watching the stagnant water drown.

Oh, the land is bleak and bare,
And its soil no longer there.
Doesn't anybody really care?
I ask for better in my prayers.

You can help us out.
Just get up, out and about.
Be a planet scout.
Take time to bellow, and time to shout.

Oh, must be something in the water
Causing its colour to alter.
The oceans seem to rise and falter,
From the Antarctic to the rock of Gibraltar.

Oh, we can do better –

Demonstrate or write a letter.

Go solo, be a go-getter.

Make the rain shine, and the sun wetter.

Oh, it doesn't have to be so bad.

If we work together,

We won't need to be so sad.

We'll make the planet better.

You can help us out.

Just get up, out and about.

Be a planet scout.

Take time to bellow, and time to shout.

Spid felt sad when he'd finished writing. How could everyone be making such a mess of the planet? After all, they only had one. To survive, they needed to protect it. They had to stop damaging it with plastic and rubbish. And stop poisoning the air with pollution. Otherwise ... well, Spid couldn't bear to think what might happen.

He stood up. "Ready, everyone?"

"Ready!" the gang replied.

"Good," Spid said. "Because it's time to go and sort out our corner of the planet."

At the little roundabout, the spidlings quickly hid themselves in the bushes in the middle. Rid, Stid and Cleverley Evaleigh had their phones at the ready to take pictures and videos of litter-spids. Spid, Bid and Herman used binoculars to spot any spidlings throwing rubbish out of their car windows further away.

Half an hour passed ...

Lots of spidlings drove by in their cars and vans, but not one of them threw out any rubbish.

"Not to worry," said Herman. "Someone will throw something out soon. It must be nearly lunchtime. There'll be burger boxes and Arachno-Cola cans everywhere."

Spid rubbed his tummy. "Did you have to mention burger boxes and Arachno-Cola cans? I'm actually getting rather hungry."

"Me too," said Herman. "But we need to stay put. When a litter-spid litters, we've got to be here to catch it on camera."

Rid looked in his bag and found a silverfish sandwich right at the bottom. "You can share this if you like, Spid," he offered. But as he couldn't be sure how long the sandwich had been there, Spid decided he'd rather go hungry.

Another half-hour passed. There were still no litter-spids in sight.

"This is hopeless," Spid moaned. "In fact it's worse than that – it's litterless."

"Being litterless is rather a good thing, isn't it?" said Bid.

"Not when you're trying to catch litter-spids it's not," Spid replied. "How are we going to get spidlings in Spider Webdon to understand the problem when we can't actually show them any litter-spids causing it?"

Cleverley Evaleigh said, "Perhaps we should go back to Herman's house and make a different plan."

"There isn't time," Spid said. "If we do that, we'll end up wasting the rest of the day. We need to take action and we need to do it now."

"Wait ..." Herman lifted a foot and looked lost in thought.

"Wait for what?" asked Stid.

"Ssh ..." said Herman. "I think I'm getting an idea ..." A moment passed. "Yes ... yes, I'm definitely getting an idea." And he put his foot back down on the ground.

"Well, what is it?" said Spid. By now, he felt quite grumpy – partly because their plan wasn't working and partly because he was hungry.

"Indeed ," replied Herman. "You see, Spid, what it is, is this. We've been so busy looking for litter-spids that we've forgotten something very important. We've forgotten about the fly-tippers."

"Litter-spids. Fly-tippers. What difference does it make? There still aren't any on this roundabout."

"Aha," replied Herman. "But a sofa, fridge and mattress were fly-tipped in the gateway to Farmer Spidcrop's farm only last week. I had to move them with my tractor and take them to the disposal site. Only, when I got there, the site was closed. So, guess what? They're still in my tractor."

"So?" Spid snapped.

"So," said Herman, "if I go and fetch them, we can dump them in the road just here to make a road block. Then we can sit on the sofa and the mattress and refuse to move. When the shops close and all those shopping spidlings try to leave Spider Webdon in their cars, they won't be able to."

Spid felt even more grumpy. "But how will that help? All it'll do is cause a huge traffic hold-up."

"I know," said Herman. "Just think about that. It'll be so huge that we're bound to be on the TV news. Then, when we've got everyone's attention, we'll be able to tell them what a bad state the planet is in. We'll be able to let them know that we all need to do our bit to help by throwing litter and plastic away properly and recycling whatever we can."

STOP
THINK
BAG IT AND BIN IT
SAVE OUR PLANET
BAG IT AND BIN IT
SAVE OUR PLANET

Spid instantly looked brighter. "Do you know what?" he said. "I think that might just work. Well done, Herman! Another spidtastic idea. The only problem is, the shops will be closing before too long. How are you going to get all the way back to your house, fetch your tractor *and* drive it back here in time?"

"Easy," Herman said. "I'll run. Really fast."

Spid said, "I thought you said you fall over when you run really fast."

"Not always. Besides, this is an emergency. So if I do fall over, I'll just get back up and start running again."

Before Spid could say another word, Herman was off. And even though he must have tripped over his own seven feet several times, he was back at the roundabout in his tractor surprisingly quickly.

Brakes squeaking, he parked in the middle of the road and pulled a lever. Then the big bucket at the front of the tractor lowered the sofa, mattress and fridge to the ground.

Stid quickly ran over and felt about down the back of the sofa cushions.

Spid frowned. "What are you doing?"

"Checking for money," Stid replied. "Things fall out of pockets when you're sitting on a sofa. You never know what you might find ... Aha!" With that, he pulled out a ten spid-quid note. "Told you," he said. "There's money in rubbish, you know!"

Herman chipped in, "That's absolutely right. There is money in rubbish. Not necessarily stuffed behind a cushion, but bigger things like furniture can be sold. And if that fridge is still in working order, it could be sold too – or even given away to someone who needs it.

"And as for that old mattress, it's got plenty of springs inside it which a scrap metal merchant would be happy to buy. What a waste to dump it all in a country lane. So bad for the environment too."

Herman and Spid pushed the furniture into a line to form a block across the road.

"Now what?" asked Bid.

"Now," said Herman, "we make ourselves comfy."

So Herman, Spid and Bid sat down on the sofa, while Rid and Stid perched on the mattress. Cleverley Evaleigh stood next to them, ready to film everything that happened.

In no time at all, a car drove up.

"What's going on?" demanded the spidling in the driver's seat. "You can't block the road up like this. I'm a solicitor, I know these things. Please clear the way so I can get by."

STOP THINK
BAG IT
BIN IT
BAG IT
BIN IT

"I'm very sorry, madam," said Spid, "but we're staying put. This is a non-violent protest against littering. We want to make the spidlings of Spider Webdon aware of the harm they're doing to the environment."

"Well, you're right about that," said the spidling in the driver's seat. "Littering is dreadful for the environment. I'm a solicitor, I know these things. Rula Law's the name."

With that, Rula Law got out of her car. "Tell you what – I'll join you. Move over on that sofa!"

As she sat down, Rula took out her phone. "Let's make this REALLY big. The more spidlings who hear about it, the better. I shall ring Spider Webdon's Spy TV and the Spider Webdon *Enquirer*. They both like a good story and they'll love this one. Not only that," Rula added, "I'll get to be on television!"

There was now quite a queue of cars lined up behind Rula's. Some of the drivers tooted their horns. Others looked angry and shouted things like, "Get out of my way, or I'll blast you to the moon!" But Spid, Herman and Bid had been to the moon, so that didn't worry them.

All of a sudden, Herman said, "Spid – gang – we need to start chanting. We need to let these spidlings know why we're blocking the road. Say what I say – and keep saying it."

Herman stood up and faced the growing line of cars. Then, in a loud, strong voice he said:

"NO MORE LITTER. STOP DESTROYING THE PLANET.
NO MORE LITTER. IT REALLY IS TIME TO BAN IT.
BAG IT. BIN IT. BAG IT. BIN IT."

BAG IT
BIN IT
STOP
THINK
SPID
THE SPIDER
BAG IT AND BIN IT
SAVE OUR PLANET

He said it again. Then again. Then Spid jumped up and started to chant it with him. Bid, Rid and Stid quickly joined in. Cleverley Evaleigh did too, although a little more quietly as she was still filming with her phone.

Even Rula Law chanted along, as soon as she'd finished ringing the *Enquirer* newspaper and the TV station.

Some spidlings were still angry. But, to the gang's surprise, once others heard their chanting and realised what the protest was about, they started to cheer and to chant along as well.

In no time at all, reporters had turned up – and not just from the *Enquirer* and Spider Webdon's Spy TV. There were reporters from other TV stations and newspapers too, and from the radio. And they all wanted to interview Herman and Spid!

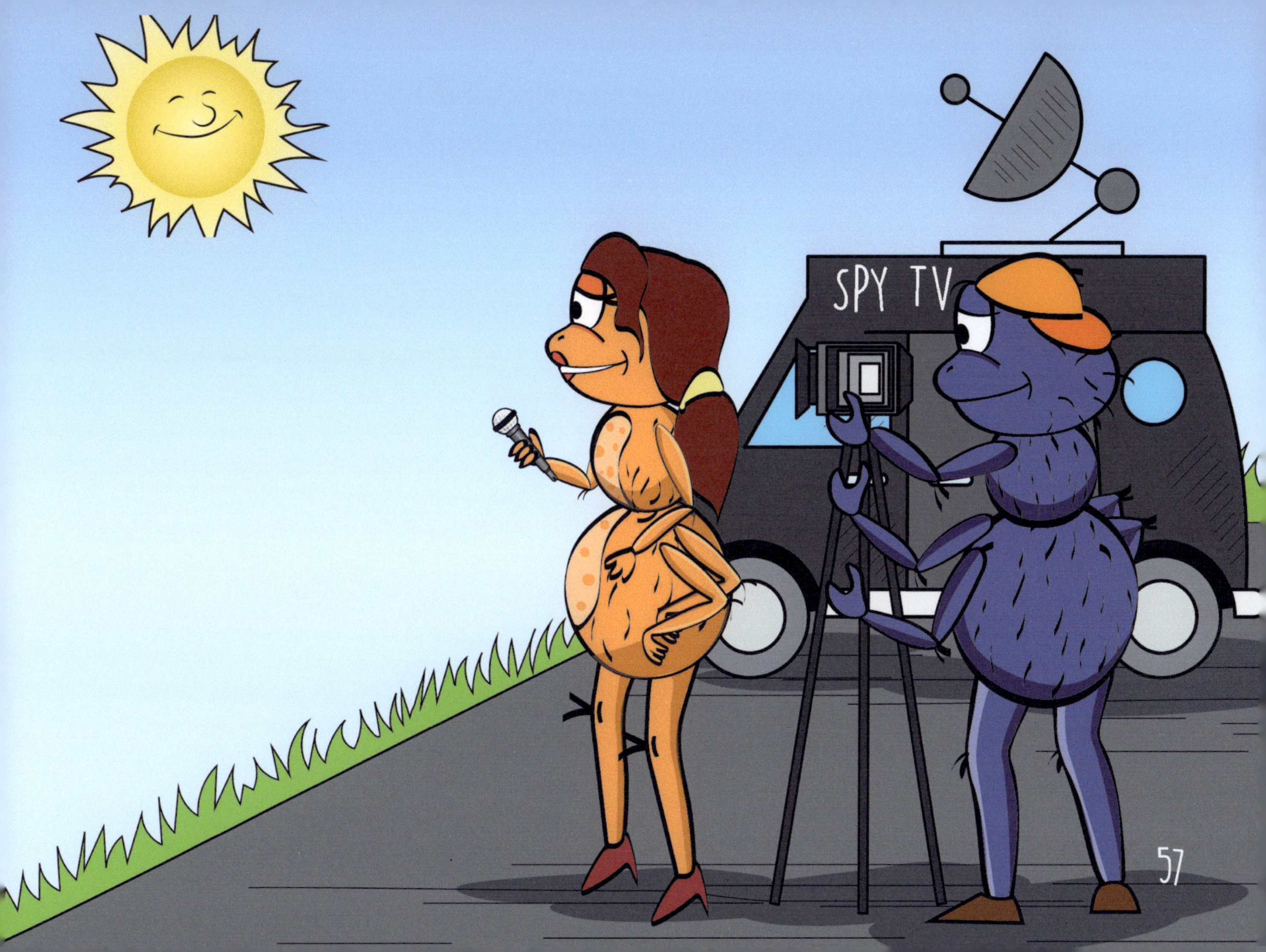
SPY TV

"Great spidding sausages!" cried Spid. "Your road block idea has worked a treat, Herman. We'd never have attracted this much attention with a few photos of litter-spids."

"I think you're right," Herman agreed. "Spidlings are going to hear about this far and wide. Which is spidtastic, because hopefully it will make them think twice before they drop litter far and wide."

As the queue of cars grew longer and longer, and the chanting grew louder and louder, a rather important-looking spidling arrived.

Bid nudged Spid. "Look! It's Sir Brown-Envelope! He's bound to be able to help. After all, he's very important-looking."

When Spid and Herman had finished explaining what their protest was about to the reporters, they explained the same thing to Sir Brown-Envelope.

"Litter is clogging up our streets and our waterways," said Herman. "This furniture right here was just dumped in one of Farmer Spidcrop's gateways."

"It was," said Spid. "And it's got to stop. All this rubbish is ruining our planet."

"I see," said Sir Brown-Envelope. "Well, all I can say is ..."

"Yes?" said Spid and Herman together.

"... You're absolutely right! In fact, I'm going to talk to Spidland's Minister for Litter to see if we can't make some sort of new law to stop this from happening. You see, you can be given a fine here if you're caught dropping litter. But in the country of Singapore, it's actually against the law to drop rubbish. And guess what? Singapore is one of the cleanest places on the planet. No, it's time to take action. And action I shall take!"

Herman looked amazed. "Really?" he said. "You'd really do that? For us?"

Sir Brown-Envelope gave a loud snort. "Not for you, no!" he bellowed. "I'll do it for the planet!"

"Erm," Spid began, "if you do make a new law, could you please call it 'Spid's Law'? After all, it was me who started the campaign."

"Don't you think it should be called 'Herman's Law'?" Rid said. "I mean, if it wasn't for Herman's road-block plan, no one would even be thinking of making a new law."

Before Spid could argue, Cleverley Evaleigh said, "Why not call it the 'Spid-Herman Law' – because Spid got us all thinking about the problem and Herman put the plan together."

Spid beamed. "I knew we could rely on Cleverley Evaleigh to come up with something cleverley."

"I was actually just about to suggest the 'Spid-Herman Law' myself," Bid said, looking put out.

"Of course you were," said Spid.

"Right," said Rula Law, "now that's all sorted, we really do need to get this traffic moving."

"Good point," said Spid. "But what are we going to do with the old furniture?"

"Simple," Rula replied. "You know the centre for homeless spidlings on the other side of Spider Webdon? They're always looking for things like this. You can drop it off there and they'll be delighted. I'm a solicitor, I know these things."

"Marvellous idea," said Herman. "Not only will we be recycling, we'll be helping other spidlings too."

Some of the spidlings at the front of the traffic queue offered to help put the furniture back into Herman's tractor. Others came up and shook hands with Herman, Spid and the gang.

"Well done, all of you," they said. "We think you're all heroes."

Spid grinned. Herman blushed. And when the gang finally got back to their homes after their long and tiring day, they all knew they'd done something really special.

So special, in fact, that Spid didn't go to bed until late. He had another song buzzing round in his head, and the words were too important not to write them down straight away ...

THE ECO SONG (BAG IT, BIN IT)

Bag up your trash,
Help the ecosystem last.
Make some lovely cash,
And build up your stash.

Clear out your rubbish.
Even though you love it,
You need to rise above it
In your ecosystem summit.

Bag it, bin it,
Put your rubbish in it.
It's not trash, it's trade cash –
It'll be all over in a minute.

Clean up your water.
Be a liquid lawyer.
Like a dark destroyer,
Be the earth's employer.

Don't ever despair,
Refresh your clean air.
Put oxygen in repair
With nature's fanfare.

Bag it, bin it,
Put your rubbish in it.
It's not trash, it's trade cash –
It'll be all over in a minute.

Protect your land,
It's always in demand.
Take a second glance
Before it turns into sand.

Use it, don't abuse it,
Or you will lose it.
Your choice is choose
Not to excuse or refuse it.

Bag it, bin it,
Put your rubbish in it.
It's not trash, it's trade cash –
It'll be all over in a minute.

Bag it, bin it,
Put your rubbish in it.
It's not trash, it's trade cash –
It'll be all over in a minute.

SPID
THE SPIDER

You can listen to these songs on Spid's website and on his second album, *The Fun Goes On*. They are also available from all good music stores.

Spid the Spider returns in
Spid the Spider Investigates a Mystery at Easter